THE RATS

A Play in One Act

by

AGATHA CHRISTIE

SAMUEL FRENCH

FRENCH

LONDON

NEW YORK TORONTO SYDNEY HOLLYWOOD

THE RATS

Presented by Peter Saunders at the Duchess Theatre, London, on the 20th December 1962, with the following cast of characters:

(in the order of their appearance)

SANDRA GREY	*Betty McDowall*
JENNIFER BRICE	*Mercy Haystead*
DAVID FORRESTER	*David Langton*
ALEC HANBURY	*Raymond Bowers*

Directed by HUBERT GREGG

Setting by PETER RICE

SCENE: *The Michael Torrances' flat in Hampstead*

Time—the present

THE RATS

SCENE—*The Michael Torrances' flat in Hampstead. A fine summer evening about 6.30 p.m.*

The flat is of the one-roomed modern type. A long window runs right across the back showing a view over the roof-tops. At the R *of the window a door leads out to a small balcony. There is a door up* L *leading to the bathroom and kitchenette. The entrance door to the flat is down* R. *In the middle of the window* C *is a very big chest of the type known as a Kuwait Bride Chest, dark wood studded with brass nails and ornamental hammered brass and copper. Prominent is a line of Baghdad coffee-pots with large spouts (beaked) There are one or two pieces of Persian or Islamic pottery, a Kurdish knife and Baghdad sugar hammer about. Otherwise the furnishing of the flat is severely modern. A big double divan, covered with cushions, is* L, *and a low plywood table* RC *with light modern armchairs either side of it. On the table is a tray with drinks and a few glasses. There is a pouffe down* C *and a budgerigar in a cage up* C. *Modernistic patterned rugs are on the floor.*

When the CURTAIN *rises, the room is empty. The lights fade up from Black-Out. Then a buzzer and knocker sound on the door* R. *This is repeated impatiently. Then* SANDRA'S *voice cries out.*

SANDRA. Anyone there? Anyone at home? (*She knocks on the door and gives a surprised exclamation as it opens*)

(SANDRA *enters* R. *She is a smart and very attractive woman of thirty, conscious of her own sensual attractions*)

Pat—Michael? (*She crosses above the table to the door* L, *exits, re-enters, crosses back to the door* R, *looks out, moves to the terrace and looks over the balcony. Then she moves back to behind the chair* LC, *puts her wrap over the back of it, sits down on the chair* LC, *takes off her gloves and puts them in her handbag. She reaches*

*for the cigarette-box on the coffee-table, finds it empty and replaces it.
She takes a cigarette-case and lighter from her handbag, lights a
cigarette, replaces the case and lighter in the bag and places the bag
on her chair)* How extraordinary! *(She gets up and walks about,
puffing nervously with increasing irritability and glancing at her
watch)* Nice manners, I must say. *(She goes on to the terrace)*

(There is the sound of a key in the lock of the door R, *trying to
turn it. Then* JENNIFER *speaks outside in a surprised voice)*

JENNIFER. Oh, it's open! *(She pushes the door and enters)*

*(*JENNIFER *is a vacant-faced young woman of thirty-odd, a
bit of a cat and not so silly as she seems. She has rather an
affected manner. She takes her key out of the Yale lock, puts it in
her handbag, crosses above the chairs, sees the wrap, stops and
turns towards the terrace)*

Hello, Sandra.
SANDRA *(re-entering the room)* Jennifer—haven't seen you
for ages.
JENNIFER. What are you doing here?
SANDRA. I'm like you—too early for the party. *(She
crosses to the chair* R) It's always so shaming to be early, isn't
it? *(She sits)*
JENNIFER. What's this about a party? Whose party?
SANDRA. Well, not a party exactly. The Torrances just
said come in for drinks.
JENNIFER *(surprised, moving between the chairs)* They asked
you in for drinks *today?*
SANDRA. Why not? *(Sharply)* Isn't that why you're here?
JENNIFER. Not exactly. *(She turns away, amused)*
SANDRA. Why shouldn't the Torrances ask me in for
drinks?
JENNIFER *(crossing to the* R *edge of the divan)* No reason at
all—*(she pauses)* if they'd been in England.
SANDRA. Do you mean they're not in England?
JENNIFER. Unhmm. *(She nods)* They're at Juan. *(She
places her bag on the divan and sits at the* R *end of it)*
SANDRA. But Pat Torrance rang me up on Tuesday, the
day before yesterday.

JENNIFER (*mockingly*) Did she?

SANDRA (*sharply*) Yes.

JENNIFER (*coolly*) Oh, really, darling! You must do better than that. It's never any good sticking to a story that won't jell.

SANDRA. Really, Jennifer!

JENNIFER (*laughing*) I suppose you got Pat Torrance to lend you the key of the flat. (*She eyes her keenly*) And you're meeting someone here! Who is it? You might tell me. Or shall I try and guess?

SANDRA. You're talking absolute nonsense. I told you, Pat Torrance rang me and asked me to come . . .

JENNIFER (*picking up her bag*) Oh, darling! *Not* all over again! Think of something better. (*She looks at the cage*) Perhaps she asked you to come in and feed the budgerigar?

SANDRA (*doubtfully, sitting forward in her chair*) As a matter of fact—she—she did mention . . .

JENNIFER (*laughing*) But I'd already agreed to feed the little brute for her. (*She takes a packet out of her bag, rises, and crosses to L of Sandra. Reading the label*) Lovabud Budgie Food. *Your Budgie will simply love it.* (*She looks at the cage, then mockingly at Sandra*) How forgetful of Pat to ask two of us to do the same thing.

(SANDRA *rises, picks up her wrap and bag, crosses to L of the divan, and puts the bag down on it*)

SANDRA (*angrily*) Oh, really, Jennifer . . .

JENNIFER. Oh, don't be cross. I'm only teasing. It's so lovely, catching one's friends out. (*She crosses to the coffee-table and sits on the L end of it*) But you might just tell me who he is. I swear I'll be as silent as the grave.

SANDRA (*flicking her cigarette ash into the ashtray on the cabinet*) That'll be the day!

JENNIFER. Now, don't lose your temper, sweetie. What really surprises me is that the Torrances should aid and abet. I've always found them rather strait-laced. I put it down to living abroad so much in remote outposts of what used to be Empire. (*She rises, kneels on the pouffe LC and goes on coaxingly*) Sweetie, do tell me who it is you're having an affair with.

SANDRA (*turning to Jennifer*) I'm not having an affair with anyone.

JENNIFER. Then why are you here in the Torrances' flat when they're in the South of France—telling silly fibs about a cocktail party?

SANDRA. There must have been some mix-up or other—you know how things are on the telephone. Perhaps Pat meant *next* week. (*She crosses above Jennifer to the chair* R) But I can tell you that I came here expecting to find a party and that's all there is to it.

JENNIFER (*disappointedly, sitting on the pouffe and facing Sandra*) And you're really and truly not expecting to meet anyone here?

SANDRA (*turning to face Jennifer*) The only person I'm actually expecting to meet here is John.

JENNIFER. Your husband?

SANDRA (*flicking her ash into the tray on the coffee-table*) Yes. He said he'd join me here as soon as he could get away from the office.

JENNIFER. Dear John. Such a pet, isn't he?

SANDRA (*smiling as she sits in the chair* R) Naturally I think so.

JENNIFER. Such a nice, simple, *trusting* man! He simply worships you, doesn't he?

SANDRA. He doesn't actually dislike me.

JENNIFER. What splendid understatement! Men don't usually dislike you, do they? Quite the contrary.

SANDRA (*coldly*) Hadn't you better feed the budgerigar if that's really what you've come for?

JENNIFER (*rising to* L *of Sandra*) Sandra! Are you suggesting that I came here to meet someone?

SANDRA. Certainly not! I should never dream of such a thing.

JENNIFER. Well, that really is a bitchy thing to say! (*She moves up to the cage, sits on the chest, opens the cage door, takes out the tray, closes the door, and fills the tray from her packet*) Tweet, tweet, tweet, here you are, then! Luvabud for the budgie. You know, there's something rather non-U about a budgie, don't you agree? But then there's something terribly non-U about the Torrances. All this travelling about to strange places and bringing back souvenirs. I stole an ashtray from the Carlton in Cannes once, but I never forgave myself. (*She replaces the seed tray and closes the cage*) And why only one bird, why not two? Look at the poor little mite, all shut up in one room and simply pining for a mate. (*She looks at Sandra*) But then, if there were two of you, you'd have to be faithful, wouldn't you? Such a bore. My God, he's drunk his own weight in water since this morning. (*She opens the cage, removes the water dish, closes the cage and moves to the door* L) Never mind, mother will get you some more—or do you suppose he'd rather have gin? If it is **a** he! (*She looks back at the cage*) How do you tell?

(JENNIFER *exits* L.

SANDRA *rises and moves to the terrace.*

JENNIFER *re-enters, having filled the water dish. She replaces it in the cage and closes the door, then picks up the seed packet from the chest*)

What are you doing out there, darling? No good looking for the Torrances. I tell you they're abroad. Or perhaps you weren't looking for the Torrances. (*She moves to the divan and replaces the packet in her bag*) Well, that's my chore done for the day, and I'm going. Good-bye, Sandra.

SANDRA (*crossing to the divan for her wrap*) I'll come with you. No point in my staying, obviously.

JENNIFER. But what about John? He'll be coming.

SANDRA. Oh, John—well, he can . . .

(*The buzzer sounds*)

JENNIFER. I expect that's him now. (*She crosses to open the door* R, *standing behind it*)

(DAVID FORRESTER *enters* R. *He is a good-looking man of about thirty-eight. Behind his charm and manner, you sense a certain hardness and ruthlessness. An ambitious man. On seeing the two women he looks taken aback, but quickly masks his surprise.*

SANDRA, *on the other hand, displays real astonishment*)

DAVID. Hullo, Sandra.

SANDRA. David!

JENNIFER (*coming from behind the door*) Hullo!

DAVID. Hullo.

SANDRA (*moving in to* R *of the divan*) Er—Mr Forrester—Mrs Brice.

JENNIFER (*offering her hand*) How do you do?

DAVID (*shaking her hand*) How do you do?

SANDRA (*quickly*) You seem to have come on the wrong day, David—like me. Jennifer has just been telling me the Torrances are abroad.

DAVID (*crossing to between the chairs*) Really. (*He smiles at Jennifer*) That seems to make three of us.

JENNIFER (*indicating the cage*) Oh, I just came in to feed the budgerigar.

DAVID (*vaguely; looking at the bird*) Oh, I see. Nice little fellow. (*He moves up to the cage*) Does he talk?

JENNIFER. Only Swahili.

DAVID. Very expressive language, I've always understood.

JENNIFER. Well, I must fly. So nice to have seen you. (*She looks towards Sandra maliciously*) Good-bye, darling.

> (JENNIFER *exits* R. DAVID *crosses to above the coffee-table to put down his hat.*
> JENNIFER *re-enters*)

Give my love to John, won't you? It's all been the greatest fun.

> (JENNIFER *exits* R, *closing the door*)

DAVID. Who the devil was that?

SANDRA. Jennifer Brice.

DAVID. Friend of yours?

SANDRA (*turning away towards the cabinet down* L) I wouldn't say so.

DAVID. What was she doing here?

SANDRA (*stubbing out her cigarette in the ashtray on the cabinet*) You heard her. She came to feed the budgerigar. Whatever are you doing here?

DAVID. Darling—I came to see you.

SANDRA (*turning to him*) Me?

DAVID (*turning up stage*) By the way, whose flat are we in?

SANDRA. The Torrances'.

DAVID (*enlightened*) Oh, I see. (*He looks round*) Well, it's very nice and suitable. (*He smiles and crosses to the divan*) Do both the Torrances sleep on this? Surely not.

SANDRA. I think it opens into a double.

DAVID. That's kind of it. Sandra . . . (*He kisses her passionately*)

SANDRA (*responding*) David . . .

DAVID. It's been quite a while.

SANDRA. Too long!

(DAVID *kisses her*)

DAVID. All of a week!

SANDRA. No. Monday—at the theatre . . .

DAVID (*embracing her*) That wasn't what I meant.

(*They sit on the divan*)

Has it been long for you, too?

SANDRA. An age. I wish we didn't have to be so secretive.

DAVID. Well, we do.

SANDRA. All this plotting and planning. It's such a bore.

DAVID (*suddenly disengaging himself*) It won't always be like this—but just for now . . . That woman—damned awkward her butting in like that. What does she think?

SANDRA. About us?

DAVID. Yes.

SANDRA. Well—I'm afraid . . .

DAVID. She'll go away and talk, eh? What damned bad luck. We've been so careful up to now.

SANDRA. I told her I was expecting John to pick me up here.

DAVID. Did she believe you?

SANDRA (*dryly*) She might have done—if you hadn't walked in.

DAVID (*rising*) As I said—damned bad luck. (*He crosses towards the balcony door*) I must say you did a very good job of looking surprised.

SANDRA. But I was surprised.

DAVID (*turning to her*) How could you be, when you'd asked me to come?

SANDRA. *I didn't ask you to come.*

DAVID (*taking it in*) You didn't?

SANDRA. No.

DAVID. But I got a message.

SANDRA (*rising*) What message?

DAVID (*moving to* R *of* C *chair*) Would I meet Mrs Grey at five hundred and thirteen Alberry Mansions at six-thirty —this *is* Alberry Mansions, isn't it?

SANDRA. Of course it is.

DAVID. Well, then?

SANDRA (*crossing to the chair* C *and sitting on the downstage arm of it*) David—there's something very queer about all this. The Torrances rang up and asked me to come here for drinks.

DAVID. Here we go again. Who are the Torrances?

SANDRA. Michael and Pat. Just come home from the Middle East or Africa or somewhere. United Nations, UNESCO—that sort of thing.

DAVID (*turning up stage, looking at the pottery, etc.*) Obviously. All the right trappings. So—the Torrances rang you up and asked you for drinks—and you came. Obviously it's the wrong day. No signs of preparation for a party. (*Struck by a sudden idea*) How did you get in?

SANDRA. I rang—and then I found the door wasn't locked. The catch on the Yale was down.

DAVID (*crossing to the door and examining the lock*) So it is. That's peculiar.

SANDRA. It's very peculiar. And the most peculiar thing of all is that the Torrances went to the South of France last Saturday, so how on earth could Pat Torrance ring me up the day before yesterday?

DAVID (*moving in to above the coffee-table*) She rang you up herself? It wasn't a message?

SANDRA. No, it was Pat—at least I thought it was.

DAVID. But now you're not so sure? Did you recognize her voice?

SANDRA. I don't know her awfully well. She said, "Pat

Torrance speaking." It never occurred to me that it wasn't her.

DAVID (*moving above her to* L *of the pouffe*) There's something behind all this that I don't understand.

SANDRA. I don't, either. And I don't like it.

DAVID (*moving to* L *of her*) But what's the point of it all? Ringing you up, pretending to be Pat Torrence, getting you to come here, getting me to come here by sending me a message—supposedly from you. What does it all add up to?

SANDRA. I wonder . . . (*She breaks off*)

DAVID (*looking at her keenly*) You've got some idea about it. Come on, tell me.

SANDRA (*slowly*) I wondered if—it might not be—John

DAVID (*astonished*) John?

SANDRA. Sometimes I've thought—that he'd begun to suspect—about us.

DAVID (*sharply*) You never told me.

SANDRA. I thought I was probably imagining it.

DAVID (*thoughtfully; moving to the cabinet*) John . . . But how would he tie up with the Torrances? Could he have got this Torrance woman to ring you up and . . .

SANDRA. That's absurd. John hardly knows her.

DAVID (*moving to below* R *of the divan*) He might have managed to borrow their flat, and then got someone or other to ring up and pretend to be Patricia Torrence . . .

SANDRA. But why? Why?

DAVID. My dear girl, use your head. To catch us in the act. *In flagrante delicto.*

SANDRA. Oh, I see.

DAVID (*moving up* L) Perhaps he's got a couple of bowler-hatted private detectives hiding in the bathroom.

(DAVID *exits up* L. SANDRA *rises.*
    DAVID *re-enters*)

Couldn't even hide a bowler hat in there. (*He crosses above the chairs to down* R) And this place is as bare as your hand. (*Crossing below the coffee-table to below the divan*) Probably means to come here himself and surprise us in amorous play!

SANDRA. What a beastly—disgusting thing to do!

DAVID (*amused*) No good taking such a high and moral tone, darling. After all, a husband is justified, I suppose, in being annoyed if he finds his wife has taken a lover. (*He sits on the divan*) How long have you been married now?

SANDRA (*crossing below the table to R of it*) Three years.

DAVID. And old John is still inclined to be on the jealous side, eh?

SANDRA (*turning to David*) Of course he's jealous, you know that. But on the other hand he's frightfully simple. Anyone could deceive him. (*She moves below the chair R*) I was quite sure he hadn't got a clue—until just lately.

DAVID. Well, I suppose some kind friend has been around and told him the good news, though I must say we've always been careful enough.

SANDRA (*bitterly; sitting in the chair R*) Somebody always knows.

DAVID. Yes. (*He rises and moves to L of Sandra*) Well, in that case I think the best thing to be done is for us to—beat a hasty retreat. We'll meet at the usual place tomorrow—but be sure you're not followed. We certainly can't risk anyone . . . Get your things.

(SANDRA *rises and crosses to below the divan.* DAVID *reaches for his hat on the table.*

The buzzer sounds)

SANDRA (*in a low voice*) Who do you think . . .

DAVID. Ssh! (*He crosses to Sandra, putting his hat on the cabinet*) If it's John and he doesn't hear anything he'll go away again.

(*The buzzer sounds again*)

SANDRA. The door—it's open.

DAVID. I wish I'd put the damned catch down.

(*He seats* SANDRA *on the divan*)

For God's sake try to relax. Here, have a cigarette. (*He offers her a cigarette from his case*) Go on!

(SANDRA *takes a cigarette.* DAVID *lights it for her, takes*

and lights one for himself, exhales, moves to above the chair C,
turns to Sandra and shrugs.

ALEC enters R. *He is a young man of twenty-eight or nine,
the pansy type, very elegant, amusing, inclined to be spiteful. He
has a very artificial manner and is dressed in the height of fashion
—even wearing gloves)* 2ⁿᵈ Sandra & David

Alec!

ALEC. Hullo, David. Hullo, Sandra. Darlings, how
devastating. We three seem to be much too early for the
party.

SANDRA (*relieved, rising and moving to between the chairs,* R *of
David*) There is a party, then? We were just wondering.

ALEC (*crossing below the coffee-table to below the divan*) Yes,
it doesn't look much like it, does it? No *canapés*, no baked
meats, no olives.

(SANDRA *sits on the chair* R)

(*Turning*) I suppose the party is here? The Torrances
aren't giving it somewhere else, are they?

DAVID (*sitting in the chair* C) Well—well—we wondered.

ALEC. How long have you two been here?

SANDRA (*quickly*) Oh, I came about five minutes ago and
David has just arrived.

ALEC. Oh, I see. (*He puts his hat on the divan*) You didn't
come together.

DAVID. No.

SANDRA (*at the same moment*) No.

(ALEC *looks at them. There is a pause*)

Pat rang you, did she?

ALEC. No, it was Michael, as a matter of fact. Of course,
he is rather a vague chap. I don't know him all that well.
He just said would I roll along here to drinks six-thirty
p.m. onwards. So here I am . . .

DAVID. All dressed up!

ALEC. Well, I've been to the garden party. My dear, the
people nowadays! (*He looks round and moves to the cabinet
down* L) Anyway, I gathered this was to be quite a do.

DAVID. Did Michael say so?

ALEC. No—he just said "drinks"—(*he opens the cabinet*) but there are ways of saying things. Well, there's something. I'm sure he'd want us to celebrate. (*He picks up an almost empty whisky bottle*) Oh! (*He replaces it and picks up a gin bottle*) Ah, gin! All right? There seems to be tonic.

SANDRA. Fine.

(ALEC *pours out three gin-and-tonics*)

DAVID (*with decision; rising and moving to below the cabinet*) Well, it seems to be quite clear what's happened. The Torrances *are* giving a party, but they're giving it somewhere else and either they thought we knew where they were giving it or they forgot to say.

ALEC. It's rather queer, though, isn't it?

(DAVID *crosses to Sandra with two glasses*)

I mean, that they should have forgotten to say so to all three of us.

(DAVID *checks, then goes on to give Sandra her glass*)

(*Turning to face them, holding his glass and the tonic bottle*) Well—"Absent friends" seems the right toast. To the Torrances!

DAVID. The Torrances!

(*They drink.* DAVID *crosses to the divan and sits on the R end of it*)

SANDRA (*with elaborate pretence*) Somebody—it was Jennifer Brice, as a matter of fact——

(ALEC *replaces the tonic bottle*)

—said that the Torrances were abroad. I didn't believe her, but now I wonder . . .

ALEC. Jennifer Brice! (*He moves to L of Sandra*) Has she been here?

SANDRA. She came to feed the . . .

DAVID. Budgerigar.

(ALEC *moves up to the cage, then to below the chest, then sits on the upstage arm of the chair C*)

ALEC (*happily*) My dears, how intriguing. Now wait a minute, let me work it all out. The Torrances have gone away. Somebody else—we don't know who—has asked us three to come here. (*He rises and turns to David*) But why? Exciting, isn't it? Quite like one of those mysteries in books. (*He kneels in the chair, facing David*) Perhaps they'll expect us to hunt round for a clue—you know, that'll send us on to the next place. Yes. (*He rises and moves down stage, looking out front, then to below the divan facing up stage*) Really, what extraordinary things the Torrances have! (*He picks up a coffee-pot from the shelves above the divan*) I suppose they brought this back with them from Baghdad. Oh, what a strange nose it's got.

SANDRA. Yes, cruel.

ALEC. Darling, that's very penetrating of you. (*He replaces the pot and moves to between the chairs*) Yes, it is cruel. It's odd, isn't it, but this whole flat looks rather cruel to me. So bare and cold. These four walls that hold you in, and just the minimum of necessities to live in it. (*He crosses to R of David*) What a horrible place to be shut up in if you couldn't get out.

DAVID. It's a perfectly ordinary modern flat, Alec. Now don't start thinking up things.

ALEC. You're so hearty, David. You won't let me have any pleasant imaginings. (*He crosses to the chest*) Now this, I believe, is what is known as a Damascus bride chest. Seems to have worm in it. (*He moves to the Kurdish knife on the wall R, and removes it from its sheath*) Ough! Here's one of those bloodthirsty knives that you stab your wife with when she's been unfaithful. (*Crossing to David with the knife*) The inlay on the hilt's rather nice, isn't it, David? Well, go on. Take it. It won't bite you.

DAVID (*taking the knife*) Yes, splendid. (*He returns it to Alec*)

ALEC (*taking the knife*) You're so inartistic. (*He moves to Sandra, giving her the knife*) Don't you think it's nice, Sandra?

SANDRA (*taking it*) Beautiful. (*She hands it back to Alec*)

ALEC (*moving to the terrace with the knife*) Now, what's out here? (*He re-enters the room*) Five floors up. What a drop. (*He looks at Sandra, then moves back or to the terrace again*)

Might be a cliff in Cornwall. Perfect for suicide. Oh—
I've dropped it! (*He re-enters the room*) The knife—I've
dropped it. Not on anyone's head, fortunately. Now I
suppose I'll have to go down and pick it up. (*He moves to
below the divan and picks up his hat*) What a bore. While I'm
there I'll see if I can find a porter.

SANDRA. I don't think there is one.

ALEC. Well, there's an office. There must be a manager
or manageress. (*Crossing straight to the door* R) I'll just pop
in and find out if the Torrances are away and if they've
let this flat to anyone.

DAVID. We might as well all go . . .

ALEC (*from the other side of the door*) No. You stay here.
Finish your drinks. Make yourself at home. I shan't be
long.

(ALEC *exits* R, *closing the door and locking it*)

DAVID (*loudly and angrily; moving to the coffee-table and putting
his glass on it*) Of course that ass *would* turn up here. He's
got the most malicious tongue in London.

SANDRA. D'you think he thought it odd, the two of us
being here together? (*She puts her glass on the coffee-table*)

DAVID. I bet he did. (*He moves up to behind the chair* C)
He'll probably go around everywhere telling people that
we've got the Torrances to lend us their flat to meet in
while they're away.

SANDRA (*rising to below the divan*) We'd better go.

DAVID (*stopping her*) No, wait a minute. If we go off
together it looks bad. (*He moves to* R *of the divan*) Isn't Alec
rather a friend of John's?

SANDRA. Oh, in a way. The person Alec was really
devoted to was my first husband, Barry. He was really
terribly upset when Barry died.

DAVID. When he went over that cliff in Cornwall?

SANDRA. Yes. (*Amused*) With the fuss Alec made anyone
would think I'd *pushed* Barry over.

DAVID (*lightly*) Did you?

SANDRA. What do you mean?

DAVID (*surprised*) Nothing. (*He turns away to behind the
chair* C)

SANDRA. I jolly nearly went over myself. (*She shivers*) It was terrifying. The whole cliff subsided after a heavy rain.

DAVID (*thoughtfully*) So Alec doesn't like you very much.

SANDRA (*moving down* L *a little*) I don't think he likes any women.

DAVID. But he particularly doesn't like you?

SANDRA (*turning to David*) What are you getting at?

DAVID. I just wondered—if it could be Alec who's behind this whole thing. Getting us here, I mean.

SANDRA. But why should he?

DAVID (*following out his thought*) Getting us to meet here, and then passing the word to John to come and find us together.

SANDRA (*moving in towards him*) That's ridiculous. Anyway, if Alec had done that, why should he come here himself? That would ruin the whole point of the thing.

DAVID. Yes, yes, you're right. (*He takes the two glasses from the coffee-table to the cabinet down* L, *then crosses to the door* R, *taking his hat with him*) At any rate, we might as well get out of here now. We'll go and join friend Alec down below.

SANDRA. I must say I'd like to know the explanation of all this—it does seems so queer. (*She moves to the divan for her wrap and bag*) I can't really believe that . . .

(DAVID, *at the door* R, *rattles the handle*)

DAVID. Hullo, this door's locked.

SANDRA. Oh, I expect the latch has slipped back in the Yale.

DAVID (*turning the Yale lock handle*) No, no, it's not the Yale. You see, there's another lock below—a mortice lock. *That* seems to be locked.

SANDRA (*moving to* L *of the coffee-table*) But it can't be. We got in quite easily and . . .

DAVID (*backing down stage a pace*) Somebody seems to have locked it from the outside.

SANDRA. Locked us in, do you mean?

DAVID. Yes.

SANDRA (*moving to below* R *of the coffee-table*) But that's absurd. We can . . . (*She stops*) Who locked it?

DAVID. Alec.

SANDRA. Alec? Why should Alec lock us in? (*She moves to the door*) All we have to do is bang or shout.

(DAVID *stops her, seats her in the chair* R, *then drops his hat on the coffee-table and crosses to below the chair* C)

DAVID. No, don't do that. Wait a minute—sit down. We've got to think this out first. There's something very odd going on. It may be Alec or it may be someone else. *Somebody* got us here, pretending to you to be the Torrances, and sending me a message apparently from *you*. (*He stands between the chair* C *and the divan*) Whoever it is got us here, and now we're locked up here, together.

SANDRA. But it's absurd. We've only got to shout.

DAVID. Oh, yes, shout. And then what happens? A scandal. Here we are, meeting in somebody else's flat while they're away, obviously a guilty assignation of some kind—and then some practical joker has locked us in.

SANDRA. Then the sooner we call his bluff the better. (*She rises and crosses to the door* R) We'll make a hell of a row and pass it all off as a joke.

DAVID (*his manner getting curt and unpleasant*) I tell you I can't *afford* a scandal! (*He moves below the divan*) It'll absolutely ruin my chances of getting that appointment. If John were to bring divorce proceedings now, it'd be the end.

SANDRA. What a selfish brute you are. (*She crosses between the table and the chairs to* R *of David*) You don't think of any-one but yourself. What about me? What about my reputation?

DAVID. You've never had much of one.

(SANDRA *slaps his face*)

(*Rudely*) Sit down.

(SANDRA *sits on the divan*)

Let me think. (*He moves up to between the chairs*) Yes. Some-body laid a trap for us and we're caught in it. We've got to think of the best way out.

SANDRA. You still think it was John. I don't believe it.

DAVID (*moving above* R *chair towards the door* R) It's Alec I'm thinking of. Alec hates my guts—always has. (*He moves up to the chest*) Suppose that Alec worked upon John and . . . (*He stops abruptly, standing by the Kuwait chest, looking down at the ground*)

SANDRA. What is it?

DAVID (*kneeling at the chest, touching something on the floor*) Sawdust. A little heap of sawdust. These holes—they're not worm-holes. They've been drilled—four little round holes. (*He gets up and moves to* R *of Sandra*) Air holes, so that somebody could breathe.

SANDRA (*rising*) What do you mean?

DAVID (*taking her and swinging himself to her left, down* L) Supposing Alec worked on John's suspicions—supposing he suggested that John should hide in the chest and that he, Alec, would arrange to get us here together.

SANDRA. You mean—you mean that John's hiding now in that chest? He is there now? That he's heard all we've been saying—that—that . . .

DAVID. I think it's possible—quite possible.

(SANDRA *looks at the chest, then at David.* DAVID *moves up to the chest, opens the lid, looks inside, then closes the lid and moves to* R *of the chair* R)

My God!

SANDRA (*crossing to the chair* C) What is it? What is it? (*She moves to the chest*)

DAVID. Don't! Don't look inside!

SANDRA (*moving towards David, to* L *of the chair* R) What is it?

DAVID (*taking her and seating her in the chair* R) Come and sit down. Now, don't *scream*. Keep your voice down. (*Moving below the coffee-table to* L *of the chair* C) We've got to keep our heads over this.

SANDRA. Tell me . . .

DAVID. It's John. He's there, in that chest. And he's dead.

(*There is a pause*)

SANDRA. Dead? John?

DAVID. He's been killed. Did you do it?

SANDRA. Me? What do you mean?

DAVID. You were here when I came—you sent me a message . . .

SANDRA. Why should I kill John in a strange flat and ask you to come here?

DAVID. So that I should be in it with you, my dear. You've hinted once or twice that you'd like to marry me—and you knew divorce doesn't suit my book.

SANDRA. Do you think I want to get us both hanged for murder?

DAVID. No, you thought we'd get away with it. This is somebody else's flat, isn't it? People who are away. Who was to know that you or I had been here? There's no porter downstairs, no-one saw us come in, we've no connection with this place.

SANDRA. I might just as well say that you killed him. (*She rises*) You came here perhaps, met John, killed him, put him in that chest and then went away, watched for me to arrive, and came back.

DAVID. Oh, for God's sake don't talk such rot. (*He moves to below the* R *end of the divan*) The trouble with you is that you're so damnably stupid.

SANDRA (*furiously*) You're saying what you really think now, aren't you? None of your famous charm. You're a louse, that's what you are—a louse and a rat!

DAVID. What about you? How many men have you hopped into bed with, I should like to know?

SANDRA. You bastard! You filthy, rotten bastard! (*She moves below the coffee-table to* R *of it*)

(*The telephone rings.* DAVID *backs below the divan. They look at the chest, then* SANDRA *looks at David*)

(*In a shaking voice*) Who—who do you think it is?

(*They face the telephone*)

DAVID. I don't know.

SANDRA. Should we . . .

DAVID. I think—not.

SANDRA. It may be just Alec ringing up from downstairs.

(DAVID *goes to lift the receiver*)

No—don't.

(DAVID *stops*)

Don't.

DAVID. I can't think. I can't think. (*He sits on the divan. After a pause he rises to answer the telephone*)

(*The telephone stops.* DAVID *wipes his forehead*)

SANDRA. If that was Alec, he'll think it very odd, won't he?

DAVID. If that's Alec he'll probably come up and see. (*He pauses*) I don't think it was Alec.

SANDRA. Who do you think it was?

DAVID. I don't know. (*He moves to* R *of the pouffe*) I don't know.

(SANDRA *sits on the pouffe, facing up stage*)

I've got to think—we've got to think clearly. Somebody got us here, somebody got John here. (*He moves above the chair* C *to between the chairs*) Somebody's locked us in from outside. (*He moves to the door* R) Alec. It must be Alec. (*He goes to the chest, lifts the lid, closes it and goes on to the terrace*)

SANDRA (*rising and breaking slightly to* L) What are you doing?

(DAVID *re-enters to above the chairs*)

DAVID. D'you remember that Kurdish knife that Alec dropped over the balcony? He said he was going downstairs to pick it up.

SANDRA. What about it?

DAVID. Well, he didn't pick it up. It's still down there.

SANDRA. I don't understand.

DAVID. John was stabbed—with that knife. (*He moves towards her*) Don't you see? The pattern's getting pretty plain.

SANDRA (*wildly*) I don't see. (*She sinks to the floor, leaning on the* L *side of the pouffe*) I don't see anything. It's like a nightmare.

DAVID (*above* R *of the pouffe*) There's only one person
behind this. Alec. He told Jim that we two had arranged
to meet here and he suggested that John should bore some
air holes in that chest and hide inside it. (*He moves to above
the chair* C) Then he stabbed John and left him there. He
went away and watched for us to arrive, and then he came
back. (*Moving to* R *of* C *chair*) He drew our attention to that
knife. He had his gloves on the whole time, you remember.
He gave it to me to hold, made me take it. Then you took
it. Don't you understand? Our fingerprints are on that
knife—and there isn't a damn thing we can do about it.
Then he went away and locked the door, locking us in
with a murdered man. Two people who've the best motives
in the world for murdering him.

SANDRA. But that's crazy—crazy . . .

DAVID. Your fingerprints, and mine, on the knife—
nobody else's. And there's not a damned thing we can do
but wait for the police to arrive.

SANDRA. The police? (*She rises*) Why should the police
arrive?

DAVID (*moving to above the pouffe*) Don't you see that
logically that's bound to be the next thing that happens—
the next stage in Alec's plan?

SANDRA (*moving to below the divan, facing* L) Alec must be
mad—mad. Why should he do this to us?

DAVID. You said he was devoted to your first husband,
Barry. You've only got to take one look at Alec to see what
kind of devotion that was.

SANDRA. Well? What's that got to do with John?

DAVID (*moving to* R *of Sandra*) Did you push Barry over
that cliff?

SANDRA. Of course I didn't. I told you I . . .

DAVID (*turning Sandra to face him, and forcing her to sit with
him on the divan*) Listen, Sandra. I don't care a damn
whether you pushed him over or not. But we've got to
have this in the clear because we've got to know Alec's
reason. Did you? You were in love with John then,
weren't you, but he was a straight, simple type. Barry was
a rich man, John was poor. Divorce wouldn't have suited
you. You were out on that cliff together, you and Barry,

and the landslide happened. You saw your chance and you pushed Barry over. (*Shaking her by the shoulders*) Didn't you? Didn't you?

(SANDRA, *very vaguely, dumbly, finally nods her head*)

(*Releasing her*) And Alec knew!

SANDRA. He couldn't have known.

DAVID. Alec knew his people. (*He rises and moves to above the chairs*) He not only suspected—he was sure. He bided his time. You married John, then you got tired of John and started an affair with me. Then Alec saw his chance. To punish, as he'd put it, John and you and me. (*He turns to Sandra*) Mad—of course he's mad. The question is, what are *we* going to do now?

SANDRA (*rising and crossing below the table to the door* R) We've got to get out of here.

DAVID. Of course we've got to get out of here, but *how?*

SANDRA. We can beat on the door. We can shout.

DAVID (*circling the chair* R *to above the chair* C) What the hell good will that do us? Somebody will come and let us out, then they'll find the body and there we shall be. Hauled in for murder and a defence so fantastic no counsel would listen to it. My God, you even told that Brice woman you were *expecting* to meet John here.

SANDRA (*moving to below the chair* R) But we'll say Alec was here—we'll explain . . .

DAVID (*moving to below the divan*) Idiot! Alec will simply deny the whole thing. He had his gloves on every moment he was here. He'll deny ever having been near the place. Probably got a very pretty little alibi cooked up somewhere.

SANDRA. Somebody must have seen him come here . . .

DAVID. In a rabbit warren like this? I doubt it. (*Moving to the kitchen door*) Some way out—there must be some way out.

(DAVID *exits up* L. SANDRA *moves up stage between the chairs, nearly coming into contact with the chest. She reacts and breaks down* L.

DAVID *re-enters*)

Two damned square hygienic little boxes!

(DAVID *goes out on to the balcony.* SANDRA *moves up stage between the chairs, facing the balcony.*
 DAVID *re-enters*)

SANDRA. Isn't there a fire-escape?
DAVID. In the corridor outside, I dare say. From here there's nothing but a sheer drop. (*He crosses to the door* R) There must be some way—some way.
SANDRA. The telephone! We could ring someone up. We could say . . .
DAVID (*crossing below the table to the cabinet*) Yes, yes! Why the hell didn't I think of that before? (*He stops*) Who could we ring up? What could we say? (*He sits on the divan*)

(SANDRA *sits on the chair* R. *They look at each other, then look away.*
 The telephone rings. They look at it)

SANDRA (*after a moment or two*) Answer it! For God's sake answer it. It can't be worse than this.
DAVID. Yes. Yes, I think you're right there. (*He rises, moves to the phone, picks it up and stands there listening for a moment. He adopts a rather different voice*) Hullo? (*He puts his hand over the receiver and turns to Sandra*) It's Alec.
SANDRA (*rising*) Alec?

(DAVID *holds the receiver, listening. A voice can be heard, but not what it says. Then he drops the receiver back on the hook*)

What is it? (*She crosses to* R *of the divan*) What did he say?
DAVID. He said we were caught like rats in a trap—like the rats we are. He said that in three or four minutes the police would be arriving.
SANDRA (*with a faint scream*) Police! (*She backs up stage towards the balcony*) Police! No, no. There must be some way out.
DAVID (*moving up* C *between the chairs*) There's only one way out—through that window and down.
SANDRA. Suicide? You're mad. They'll believe what we say—we'll explain . . .

DAVID. We'll be charged with murder. We'll be convicted.

SANDRA. No! (*She looks towards the door* R *and the fanlight*) There must be some way out—there must. (*She goes to the coffee-table, sweeps it clear, takes it to the door* R *and stands on it, putting one hand through the fanlight*)

DAVID. What are you trying to do, you little fool? Claw you way out! Claw your way out!

SANDRA (*coming off the table and backing down stage towards the divan, facing David*) I didn't do it. I didn't kill John. It's all your fault. Why did I ever meet you? Why didn't you leave me alone?

DAVID (*moving to* R *of Sandra, and circling to* L *of her*) You bloody little bitch, you got me into this.

SANDRA. I hate the sight of you. I tell you I hate the sight of you. You're cold and hard and cruel and selfish as sin. You've never given a damn for anyone in the world except yourself.

(DAVID *forces her on to the divan, his hands at her throat. There is a knocking at the door* R)

VOICE. Open the door. It's the police.

(DAVID *straightens up*)

DAVID. Let them do it.

(SANDRA *rises and moves to between the chairs*)

You got away with it the first time, didn't you? But you won't get away with it this time.

(*The knocking is repeated*)

VOICE. Come on—open up!

SANDRA (*turning to face him*) I hate you.

DAVID (*circling below the chairs and Sandra to above the chairs and towards the door up* L) Or perhaps it'll be fifteen years in a prison cell. And how will you care for that?

(SANDRA *sinks on to the chair* R)

Fifteen years in a prison cell.

(*The knocking is repeated*)

VOICE. We'll break the door down.

DAVID (*backing towards the divan and below it*) Why should they come for me? It's you they should be coming for, not me. You killed Barry, not me. (*He stands by the cabinet, facing the door* R) Why the hell should I get involved?

(*A banging starts on the door—solid, steady, paced.* SANDRA *laughs hysterically, stopping as she senses the meaning of the bangs on the door*)

SANDRA. Rats in a trap, that's what we are. Rats in a trap.

The lights dim to a BLACK-OUT *and*

the CURTAIN *falls*

FURNITURE AND PROPERTY LIST

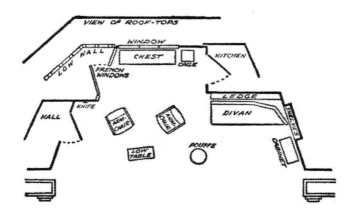

On stage :   Cabinet (down L)
        On it : telephone, ashtray
        In it :   *Top shelf :* 6 glasses, cocktail cherries
                 Bottom shelf : bottle of whisky (almost empty),
                        bottle of gin (half-full), 2 tonic splits,
                        bottle-opener, matches, corkscrew, soda-
                        syphon
     Shelves (above divan)
       Top shelf : empty
       On 2nd shelf : wooden head, illustrated vase
       On 3rd shelf : fertility god, Greek vase, Siamese lady
       On 4th shelf : two-headed vase, Roman vase
       On 5th shelf : camel head bowl, earthenware pot
     Divan. *On it :* frill, mattress, 4 cushions
              Over it : tapestry
              On shelf behind it : 3 large coffee-pots, 1 small
                  coffee-pot, 1 copper coffee-pot, 2 boxes,
                  1 bowl (ashtray) L end

Chest. *In it:* embroideries
   Under it: sawdust
Coffee-table. *On it:* ashtray, cigarette-box (empty)
2 empty chairs
Pouffe
Budgerigar cage
On floor: rugs
On wall R: light fitting. Kurdish knife in scabbard.
  Mask
Door up L, closed
Door down R, closed, latch up, fanlight closed. Check key

Personal: DAVID: cigarette-case with 2 plain and 1 tipped
       cigarettes. Lighter
    JENNIFER: handbag with birdseed and key (Yale)
    SANDRA: handbag with cigarette-case and 1 tipped
       cigarette. Lighter
    ALEC: mortice key

LIGHTING PLOT

Property fittings required: 2 wall-brackets (dressing only)

Interior. A living-room

THE APPARENT SOURCE OF LIGHT is a window up C

THE MAIN ACTING AREAS are C, up C, RC and down L

A fine summer's evening

To open: BLACK-OUT

Cue 1	At rise of CURTAIN	(Page 1)
	Fade up to daylight	
Cue 2	At end of Play	(Page 24)
	Dim to BLACK-OUT	

EFFECTS PLOT